SUMMERS FLY, WINTERS WALK

by Charles M. Schulz

An Owl Book
Henry Holt and Company / New York

Originally published in 1977 by
Holt, Rinehart and Winston, and
included strips from 1977.

Library of Congress Card Number: 77-73859

ISBN 0-8050-1692-9 (An Owl Book: pbk.)

First Owl Book Edition—1991

Printed in the United States of America

Recognizing the importance of preserving the written word,
Henry Holt and Company, Inc., by policy, prints all of its
first editions on acid-free paper. ∞

3   5   7   9   10   8   6   4

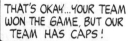

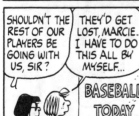

HEY, LOOK! YOUR BROTHER IS FLOATING OUT TO SEA ON THE PITCHER'S MOUND!

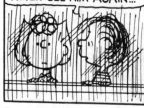
YOU SHOULD WAVE TO HIM... YOU'LL PROBABLY NEVER SEE HIM AGAIN...

SO LONG, BROTHER'!

WHO'S GOING TO FEED THE DOG?

SCHULZ

FLOATING OUT TO SEA ON A PITCHER'S MOUND... I CAN'T BELIEVE IT!

CHARLIE BROWN'S IN TROUBLE, SNOOPY... WE SHOULD DO SOMETHING...

THAT'S TRUE!

IF HE'S NOT GOING TO BE AROUND TO FEED ME ANY MORE, MAYBE I SHOULD PLANT A GARDEN...

LET'S SEE, I COULD PUT SOME TOMATOES HERE, AND SOME CORN OVER THERE AND MAYBE SOME RADISHES HERE..

SCHULZ

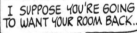

THE GIFT OF A FLOWER IS ALWAYS A GIFT OF LOVE!

HOW ABOUT ACCEPTING A FLOWER?

ACCEPTING CAN MEAN LOVE, TOO

BUT IT DOESN'T NECESSARILY HAVE TO! SOMETIMES YOU HAVE TO ACCEPT A FLOWER JUST TO KEEP FROM HURTING THE OTHER PERSON'S FEELINGS

THEN, I'LL ACCEPT IT

WHAT DOES TAKING IT BACK MEAN?

IT CAN MEAN ANY STUPID THING YOU WANT IT TO MEAN!

I'VE BEEN THINKING ABOUT SOMETHING..

CHUCK, HAVE YOU EVER TOLD A GIRL THAT YOU LIKE HER?

AND HAVE HER LAUGH IN MY FACE? NOTHING DOING!!

IT HURTS TO HAVE YOUR FACE LAUGHED IN

I DON'T UNDERSTAND, CHUCK..

WELL, SAY SOMETHING NICE TO ME, AND I'LL SHOW YOU...

SAY SOMETHING SENSITIVE TO ME AND I'LL LAUGH IN YOUR FACE..

I LIKE YOU, CHUCK

HAHAHAHA!

OW! OOO! OW! YOU WERE RIGHT, CHUCK.. MY FACE HURTS ALL OVER!

OUCH! OOO! OW! I FEEL LIKE I'VE BEEN STUNG BY BEES...

I GUESS MAYBE I'LL GO HOME

I WONDER IF THIS MEANS I'LL NEVER BE ABLE TO TELL ANYONE THAT I LIKE THEM...

IT'S BEEN TERRIBLE TALKING TO YOU, CHUCK

SIGH!

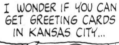

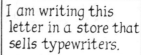

"BY THE TIME YOU RECEIVE THIS LETTER, I WILL BE ON A TRAIN HEADING FOR HOME"

"I GUESS I WON'T BE PLAYING AT WIMBLEDON AFTER ALL...I JUST HEARD THAT THEY STARTED WITHOUT ME"

ALL RIGHT FOR YOU GUYS!!

I'M SORRY YOU NEVER GOT TO PLAY AT WIMBLEDON

I WOULD HAVE WON IN STRAIGHT SETS!

DIDN'T I TELL YOU WIMBLEDON ISN'T NEAR KANSAS CITY?

I THINK THEY MOVED JUST SO I WOULDN'T GET TO PLAY!

HELLO, DAD? I JUST CALLED TO WISH YOU A HAPPY FATHER'S DAY!

WHAT?

I HAVE THE NUMBER HERE OF YOUR MOTEL, AND I JUST THOUGHT I'D SURPRISE YOU

THIS ISN'T A MOTEL

ARE YOU HAVING A GOOD TIME? ARE YOU SWINGING ANY BIG DEALS?

WHO ARE YOU CALLING?

WHAT?

I SAID, WHO ARE YOU CALLING? WHO IS THIS?

CHUCK! WHAT ARE YOU DOING THERE?

I'M NOT THERE... I'M HERE! I THINK YOU DIALED THE WRONG NUMBER...

CHUCK, YOU ALWAYS SPOIL EVERYTHING!!

I SUPPOSE SOMEDAY WHEN I GET TO BE A FATHER, IT'LL BE EVEN WORSE...

Dear Movie Critic,

How come you never like the same movies that I like?

You're weird! love, Sally Brown

Dear Television Critic,

What do you know?

You wouldn't know a good show if it bit you on the leg! love, Sally Brown

Dear Book Critic,

What's the matter, can't you read? love, Sally Brown

ANYONE IN THE MEDIA YOU WANT BLASTED?

SCHULZ

HOW WAS I TO KNOW WOODSTOCK WAS HAVING A SWIM PARTY?

SCHULZ

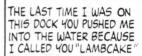

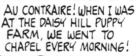

YOU WANNA HEAR A GOOD ONE?

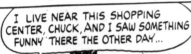

I LIVE NEAR THIS SHOPPING CENTER, CHUCK, AND I SAW SOMETHING FUNNY THERE THE OTHER DAY...

THEY HAVE A BOOK STORE AND AN ICE CREAM STORE NEXT TO EACH OTHER

THE BOOK STORE HAS A SIGN IN ITS WINDOW THAT SAYS, "PLEASE DO NOT BRING ICE CREAM INTO THE BOOK STORE"

THE ICE CREAM STORE HAS A SIGN THAT SAYS, "OKAY, THEN PLEASE DON'T BRING BOOKS INTO OUR ICE CREAM STORE"

SPEAKING OF READING AND EATING, I DON'T KNOW WHY IT IS, BUT WHENEVER I TRY TO READ A BOOK AND EAT POTATO CHIPS, MY EYES ALWAYS WATER...

I HATE TALKING TO YOU, CHUCK!

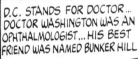

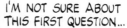

SNOOPY, I HAVE A PROBLEM...

MY DAD IS WILLING TO SEND ME TO A PRIVATE SCHOOL, BUT THEY ALL COST FOUR OR FIVE THOUSAND DOLLARS

I CAN'T ASK HIM TO SPEND THAT MUCH MONEY ON ME...WHAT SHOULD I DO?

"ACE OBEDIENCE SCHOOL... COMPLETE TRAINING.... TWENTY-FIVE DOLLARS"

I THINK I'VE FOUND A PRIVATE SCHOOL, CHUCK...

SNOOPY GAVE ME THIS BROCHURE...THEY ONLY CHARGE TWENTY-FIVE DOLLARS...

"ACE OBEDIENCE SCHOOL"?!

IT LOOKS LIKE KIND OF A FUN PLACE...

EVERY STUDENT IN THE SCHOOL SEEMS TO HAVE A PET...

I THINK YOU'RE IN TROUBLE..

PEPPERMINT PATTY THINKS SHE'S IN A PRIVATE SCHOOL... WHAT'S GOING TO HAPPEN WHEN SHE FINDS OUT SHE'S IN DOG TRAINING CLASSES?

SHE'S GOING TO COME AROUND HERE LOOKING FOR A CERTAIN BEAGLE WHO GAVE HER A BROCHURE ON THE "ACE OBEDIENCE SCHOOL"

BEAGLE? WHAT BEAGLE?

FETCH? YES, SIR!

"FETCH" MEANS TO RETRIEVE OR TO GO GET SOMETHING...

OH, I'M SORRY, SIR... I THOUGHT YOU WANTED THE DEFINITION...

THIS MUST BE THE "LEARN BY DOING" METHOD...

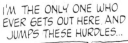

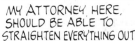

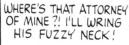

WHAT A FIGHT!

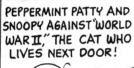

PEPPERMINT PATTY AND SNOOPY AGAINST "WORLD WAR II," THE CAT WHO LIVES NEXT DOOR!

IT'S OVER!! THE FIGHT IS OVER!!

DID WE WIN OR LOSE?

YES!

SNOOPY, OL' PAL, I OWE YOU AN APOLOGY...

THERE I WAS, ALL SET TO POUND YOU, AND YET YOU CAME TO MY RESCUE WHEN I WAS FIGHTING THAT CAT

I DIDN'T EVEN KNOW IT WAS A REAL CAT...I THOUGHT IT WAS **YOU** DRESSED IN A CAT SUIT!

NO WONDER HE WAS SO MAD...I KEPT TRYING TO PULL THE SUIT OVER HIS HEAD!

HEE HEE HEE HEE

ROUND TRIP FIRST CLASS

OCTOBER TWENTY-FOURTH

WELL, ONLY ONE MORE WEEK 'TIL HALLOWEEN, AND THEN THE..

DON'T START IN AGAIN ABOUT THE "GREAT PUMPKIN"!

IF YOU START RAVING TO ME AGAIN ABOUT THE "GREAT PUMPKIN," I'LL POUND YOU CLEAR ACROSS THE ROOM!

"A PROPHET IS NOT WITHOUT HONOR EXCEPT IN HIS OWN COUNTRY AND IN HIS OWN HOUSE"

WHAT'S THAT SUPPOSED TO MEAN?

IF I TALKED TO SOME KIDS IN A DIFFERENT NEIGHBORHOOD, I'LL BET THEY'D BELIEVE MY STORY..

WELL, GO AHEAD! TALK ALL YOU WANT, BUT JUST DON'T TALK AROUND HERE!

HI, THERE! ARE YOU AWARE THAT ON HALLOWEEN NIGHT THE "GREAT PUMPKIN" RISES OUT OF THE PUMPKIN PATCH AND BRINGS TOYS TO ALL THE GOOD LITTLE KIDS IN THE WORLD?

WEIRD!

THAT'S GOOD, BUT HOW MANY PEOPLE ARE YOU GOING TO SCARE WITH A GRAPE?

I WONDER IF WOODSTOCK PLANS TO FLY SOUTH FOR THE WINTER

I THINK HE SHOULD....

IF HE COMES BY TODAY, I THINK I'LL JUST TELL HIM THAT HE'S NOT REALLY PREPARED FOR FREEZING WEATHER, AND THAT HE...

THIS IS A STORY ABOUT MY UNCLE

MY UNCLE NEVER MISSED A DAY'S WORK IN HIS LIFE UNTIL ONE DAY WHEN HE FELL INTO A ROUTINE!

HAHAHAHA

YES, MA'AM

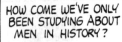

MY GRANDMOTHER LOVED TO DANCE

EVERY SATURDAY NIGHT SHE AND HER FRIENDS WENT TO THIS LITTLE PLACE THAT HAD A JUKE BOX, AND A DANCE FLOOR AND SIX BOOTHS...

SHE WAS THE FIRST ONE TO CARVE THOSE IMMORTAL WORDS ON THE BACK OF ONE OF THE BOOTHS, "**KILROY WAS HERE**"

ACTUALLY, ALTHOUGH GRANDMA WAS A LOT OF FUN, SHE WASN'T VERY CREATIVE!

AND SO, WORLD WAR II CAME TO AN END...

MY GRANDMOTHER LEFT HER JOB IN THE DEFENSE PLANT, AND WENT TO WORK FOR THE TELEPHONE COMPANY...

WE NEED TO STUDY THE LIVES OF GREAT WOMEN LIKE MY GRANDMOTHER...TALK TO YOUR OWN GRANDMOTHER TODAY... ASK HER QUESTIONS...

YOU'LL FIND SHE KNOWS MORE THAN PEANUT BUTTER COOKIES! THANK YOU!

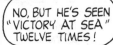

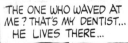